Yoga Animals So Cute

A Mindful Menagerie to Color

KIMMA PARISH

Get Creative 6

NEW YORK

Introduction

Try a new twist on the popular theme of coloring animals! Anyone who wants a bit more creativity and calm in their life will love this book featuring adorable creatures in yoga poses—dogs, cats, bunnies, elephants, foxes, sloths and more—with delightfully themed frames and scenes. There's even a page in the back with the names of basic poses! If you're into coloring and yoga, this is the book for you.

Basic Yoga Poses

Downward-Facing Dog Pose
Adho Mukha Svanasana

Easy Pose
Sukhasana

Warrior I Pose
Virabhadrasana I

Triangle Pose
Trikonasana

Tree Pose
Vrikshasana

Warrior II Pose
Virabhadrasana II

Wheel Pose
Chakrasana

Cobra Pose
Bhujangasana

Standing Forward Bend
Uttanasana

About the Author

Kimma Parish is a Florida-based artist, illustrator, graphic designer and photographer who grew up in rural Kentucky drawing inspiration from the countryside near her home. Her Etsy clipart and paper business, Le Petite Market, is highly rated with more than 39,000 sales.

Get Creative 6

An imprint of Mixed Media Resources
19 West 21st Street, Suite 601
New York, NY 10010
sixthandspringbooks.com

Editor
PAMELA WISSMAN

Art Director
IRENE LEDWITH

Designer
JENNIFER MARKSON

Chief Executive Officer
CAROLINE KILMER

President
ART JOINNIDES

Chairman
JAY STEIN

Manufactured in China

5 7 9 10 8 6 4

First Edition